# THE SPACE BETWEEN US

## NEIL ELDER

INDEPENDENT INNOVATIVE INTERNATIONAL

Published by Cinnamon Press
Meirion House
Tanygrisiau
Blaenau Ffestiniog
Gwynedd, LL41 3SU
www.cinnamonpress.com

ISBN: 978-1-78864-016-9

British Library Cataloguing in Publication Data. A CIP record for this book can be obtained from the British Library.

Designed and typeset in Palatino by Cinnamon Press. Printed in Poland.

Cover design by Adam Craig.

Cinnamon Press is represented in the UK by Inpress Ltd and in Wales by the Welsh Books Council.

# Acknowledgements

I am grateful to the editors of the following publications in which a number of these poems, or versions of them, have appeared: *Cake, The Cannon's Mouth, Clear Poetry* (online), *Envoi, The Interpreter's House, The Journal, The Poetry Shed* (online), *Prole, The Rialto, South, The Ver Prize 2016 Anthology.* The poem 'Grief Stricken' appears in *The Book of Love and Loss* (Belgrave Press). The poem 'Believers' alludes to David Bowie.

Thank you to those who have encouraged me and shown support, be they poets, family or colleagues—your kind words and interest go a long way.

I particularly want to thank Tim Gerig for his assistance, also Herga Poets, Tom Warner and Alexia Kirov, who have all been subject to early drafts and musings over time. The thoughts offered and the springboards provided have been invaluable.

Thank you to Jan Fortune, Adam Craig, Cinnamon Press and Henderson.

Finally, thanks to Ann Elder for her unflagging support throughout the years.

Also by Neil Elder:
*Codes of Conduct*—Cinnamon Press
*Being Present*—Black Light Engine Room

# Contents

*Music is the space between the notes*
*Claude Debussy*

*For Ushma, Amelia & Nathaniel—*
*who fill the spaces so beautifully.*

# The Space Between Us

# This handbook remains out of print

Swimming uphill with a snow suit on
Is not recommended for beginners.

It can be vexing to find oneself
Trailing in a stickleback wake.

The safest approach is to lie on your back
Letting the current take over.
In time you will note the point
Between silt and shore.

Intermediate persons may jump
From the bridge in order
To determine the size of their splash.

An instructor may be bankside
To offer assistance.

# Thank You for Visiting

You are now entering the gift shop.

Please take time to enjoy browsing

our range of fine quality mementos.

Among the most popular items

is a set of coasters, each featuring

high resolution images from your parents' wedding.

Tote bags with your family tree design are by the till.

You may like to purchase a snowglobe containing

a scaled replica of the house in which you grew up.

Also available is a calendar showing your first twelve years.

Our gift cards show damning comments from your school reports.

Other popular items include a set of six postcards

depicting the worst cuts and bruises you have suffered,

such as the purple mushroom shape

from when you slipped on ice, and the laceration

you received that time you came a cropper on your bike.

Address books, containing all the numbers of the people

you've lost touch with, come in three pastel shades.

Umbrellas showing copies of your X-rays

can be found on the left, just above stylish serving trays

upon which your test results have been printed.

Specially commissioned maps of your home town

are marked with every place that you have been blind drunk,

and shards of glass from the window that you put your fist through

have been laser-cut and polished to make keyrings.

Our tea-towel designs show all the women

you ever wanted to make love to,

while fridge magnets illustrated with your darkest fantasies

may also be purchased.

We are pleased to offer four limited edition fine art prints

showing scenes of how we imagine your last days,

these are situated next to the life-size cut-out

of the man you hoped to be.


We hope you have enjoyed your tour of this exhibit

and ask that you place the audio set

into one of the containers provided

on your way to the exit.

# Believers

Beneath the English evergreens that wait for you
we shadowbox our past.
The blackest of years
plays hollow through the night.

Roughed up and frightened,
we need an axe
to break strange doors
we find ourselves behind.

Look up
to keep believing,
because there's nothing else
that we can do.

# Removal

On my return the fox was gone;
replaced by sand.
The mother and child had left
as well, taking
souvenirs of fear.

A man from the council
must lift weight into a van.
That's fair,
but why not us?

Load him up,
throw down some sand,
sling him out the other end
and turn the burners on.

# 'Section Four: Treatment of Coastal Debris'

By the time I'd arrived
trophy hunters had been—
fins hacked off, teeth prised out.
Jokers too; it lay there dumbly—
bladderwrack for hair.

A high vis vest from the council appeared,
clutching clip board and notes
he read us the options.

'Leave carcass where it is,
wait a day or two for tide to take out to sea;
if unsuccessful
move to other means—
before body rots and smells.

Tow carcass out to sea and release into water.
(N.B. Travel far enough from shore
 to prevent animal from washing up again.)

Inter body, if by-laws allow;
with correct machinery you can bury on the spot.

Break carcass up and transport
to abattoir for incineration.
When no abattoir is available, dispose of in landfill.

If far enough away from homes,
and recreational beaches,
leave carcass to decompose.

It can be costly to dispose
of whales.'

# Spotlight

Shaking windows, helicopter thrum,
awake in thought-flash to strobing in your mind.
The child's bike abandoned in the park,
a phone call in the night,
the photographs you take inside your mind
each time your daughter leaves the house—
denim jacket, black leggings, t-shirt with a daisy.

Tonight someone is on the run.
Searchlight scorching grass,
floodlit gardens turning into film sets
each divided into lots.

But you've seen this one before,
they find him in the end;
behind the bins, behind the shed,
or lying in his sweat-stained bed.

# A Collectors' Piece

It could have been football programmes;
one from the Matthews' final
as the piece de resistance.

With my brother it was comics:
Marvel were king.

Or perhaps stamps, bought
and sold at fairs, followed by
long nights with Stanley Gibbons.

But for you it was eggs;
seven thousand and seven.
You had pale green and blue eggs
from blackcaps to yellow hammers,
packed-up like a Cadbury's treat.
There were blotched chestnut red eggs from ospreys,
and goshawk eggs the colour of the moon.
Which was the Faberge of the clutch —
sparrow hawk, barn owl or falcon?
Each egg logged and stored
in a collection no-one would see.

Yours was a ritual as important
as the shells themselves:
lone sorties to the farthest reaches,
times, dates and details in code —
proof of your commitment.

In the search they found your rubber dinghy and maps.
Did you fancy yourself a Victorian explorer
bringing back booty from across the globe?
A Reverend Jourdain for the modern age.

And what of the eggs themselves,
lovingly handled, blown
and nestled in cotton wool?
Much better to touch and feel their
smooth warmth and weight
than make do with pictures in a book.

When Operation Easter landed on your doorstep,
search warrants in hand,
you knew your collection was finished.
No more driving all night,
walking fifteen miles through fields of snow,
no more abseiling down crags to reach the nest.
No more to collect.

# Soundtrack

The edit plus strings
perform a strobe upon your mind.

In one take you think you've seen
nude Janet Leigh
slashed a dozen times
until you slow it down.

In *Raging Bull* Scorsese pulls a different trick;
Mascagni finds beauty in violence
La Motta smacks out seven shades
of slow-mo black and white,
and we watch wrapped
in the fling and flail of blood.
In the dark of cinemas
I try to find a soundtrack of my own.

Play the tapes again
with the sound turned down.

# At Sea

Whenever we reached the marram grass,
away from parents' eyes and pressing jumble
of the caravan park,
we knew we'd arrived.

Like corks out of bottles we raced off the dunes
in such hurry that I often missed my footing,
coming down in a buckled heap.
Leaning forwards, wrapping your hand around my forearm,
you'd always get me on my feet.

Then we'd tumble into the sea,
delighted by the shocking cold,
being sure to keep our shoulders under.

We'd drift in the current,
carried unknowingly along the shoreline,
have to swim back to where towels
made a strip of sand our own.


Now when I drift too far,
I search for you among the marram,
try to grab your hand,
try to beat the current.

# Auction Room

Bidding is slow in the auction room.
Dealers hang around at the back
hoping to be the one to spot
the sleeper nestled among silver
service no one wants
to polish anymore.

The patina of lives is rubbed away;
memories cashed in,
and objects lovingly bequeathed
gambled in an afternoon.

Today I'm biding my time;
with a bit of luck
some old boy's medals will turn up,
or a ring the grandkids thought too brash,
and the hammer will fall on the past
while I start counting the cash.

# On the Rise

Half-term and rain makes the museum
bee hive busy. But not for us
the ammonite queue that coils
its way to dinosaurs;
we're here for a picture with Darwin
looking in wisdom from the top of the stairs,
(perfect front page for school holiday project).

Photograph taken we glance about the room:
Galapagos turtles, some finches
and a dodo encased in time and glass.
Then on out of the building,
and past the egg of an elephant bird.

A tube ride away; we're along the path
thrilled by a quick flashing screech —
ring necked parakeets.
Descendents of film set escapees;
they are calling to Darwin -
*We rise, we rise.*

# Hopeful

If it did not happen today,
then perhaps it was not meant to be.
Try to accept the day for what it gave.

Even now there may be someone
writing your name on an invitation.

# A City Wakes Up

Outside the city's main gallery
students are painting copies
of the ten most cherished pieces
housed inside.

Crowds have gathered to see the students' work.
Queues form around some,
cups and caps sitting by the students' feet
become brim-full.

Yesterday, outside department stores,
the unemployed gave away
handcrafted home furnishings.
Tomorrow children shall be passing new bills
outside the town hall.

Gallery attendants pace rooms, watch clocks.
Shop assistants mind empty tills.
Councillors swallow hard.

# The Day We Lost

When the country went broke
economists worked on a kick-start
solution: a radical plan.

It was decided that costs
could be cut
by losing a day from the week.

We were told we'd save millions
with a year that was shorter
so the country united behind the idea.

A referendum was held
and the question was posed:
'Which day of the week
do you think should go?'

Some chose Monday, for obvious reasons.
Others went for Tuesday, it being neither
here nor there.

Religion meant no one could touch the weekend,
but Seventh Day Adventists,
were forced to re-brand,
while publishers prepared to revise
The Book of Genesis.

When the result was announced
live on TV, the PM declared
that Wednesday was gone.

I hung my head and put the party popper down:
Wednesday had been
my wife's one day off
and the only word I could say
in Mandarin Chinese.

# Like My Daughter Says

If, like my daughter says,
you are now a million particles
orbiting in space,
may you keep on spinning.
Or else as I look out tonight,
I hope you fall like snow
and settle for a while.

## Grief Stricken

What strikes me is the way grief
clings to you like wet clothes.
What pains me is that you have grown
into them as though they are a second skin.

I remember returning from school,
soaked through and dripping.
*Get those clothes off quick—*
*they'll be the death of you.*

# What We Could Not Give

What we could not buy were the tired nights
you sat beside our beds rubbing out life's cramps,
nor the thousand hours of sleep you never had.

And we could not find recordings
of the silent hours you bit your tongue
when you knew best to leave us be.

There was not ink enough to draw
the lengths to which you've gone for us
or to return the words of kindness you have given.

It wasn't possible to find a wall
large enough to mount a mirror that could
reflect the love that you have shown.

And there is not steel enough for girders
that can match the support
and strength that you provide.

The only thing that we can give
is the space that stands between us;
not as empty as it seems — look —
see how it glows with the warmth
and wonder you inspire.

# The Day We Learnt John Hurt Had Died

The usual fuzzy head of a Saturday morning,
kettle boiling water to a dance,
and you checking your phone.

John Hurt has died, and people are posting
lines of his
*Everyone has been ... so terribly kind*
*Christine, you're like a racehorse*
*Great men are forged in fire.*

Later, the sky recreates itself;
brackish storm clouds slashed by
sunlight turn magenta,
the colour of Quentin Crisp's hair.
And you remember -
*Vroom! Here we go. Let's become different molecules.*

# Breathing Spaces

*for Andrea Degidi*

Good weather opens our hearts,
makes the world high-resolution,
we become ourselves once more.

Heat is bringing fish into the shallows,
we count twelve before our shadows make them flick away.

Shells we find are pleasing to touch —
cool, smooth, tokens of time
to take as reminders of here.
We all want to live by the sea sometime.

Looking across the water at fishing boats,
we know tonight we'll eat the fish that they bring back,
and in the weeks ahead we'll use these days
to remind ourselves good things happen out of sight.

# Watershed During Lunch-Hour

Today she watched a man clean Jesus.
With a brush you'd use for washing up
and a plastic orange bucket,
he approached the statue stiffly.

Some half-formed religious notion told her
that he'd wash the mossy feet first,
but instead he started with the face:
top-down, the window cleaner's principle.

Perhaps a change for him from statesmen
or military figures, but from where she sat,
with her packed lunch, his swift broad strokes
seemed just too rough.

Then, as he worked around the eyes of Christ,
something changed —
the man's shoulders softened,
as though he'd heard the word *relax*.

He began to move his brush in tiny circles,
each more careful than the last;
no longer workman, but a craftsman
in the process of restoring.

And in that moment she wanted
to stand before this man,
arms outstretched in come-to-me pose,
to be cleansed and restored by his touch.

# Art Appreciation

*Fabulous.* Your amazement sticks in my mind.
But I should have guessed
your disproportionate delight
might be the start of a decline.
You were beaming as you held the vase
which I didn't know you'd kept,
just like those years before
when I'd hurried back from school
with it, my cherished gift to you.

This time, with both hands,
you place it on the sill too carefully.

Somebody's rule of inversion;
appreciation is proportional
to what is left.
Crookedly the vase leans in all its orange splendour.
I see you shake your head in disbelief
repeating *Fabulous* with wonder.

# Restoration

With chemicals, brushes and the patience of Buddha
you spend your years
in the slipstream of artistry
revealing what lies beneath.

Below tall windows
you measure time in millimetres,
edging along the folds of Mary's hem
until she glows in ultramarine.

Skimming away layers of fog
works come back into view;
you make eyes see again,
restoring the flush of life with azurite,
lapis lazuli, sienna and malachite.

Visitors to galleries stop and wonder,
but they know nothing of how your hidden strokes
have touched those of Old Masters
or of how you now long

to have just half those hunched hours back,
to be free from the fug that frames you
and paint what you see
in the life that exists outside.

# Portrait With Orange

You were eating an orange as though it were an apple
when Roddy told us he was leaving.
I could tell by the look you gave
that you hadn't seen it coming.

Wanting to keep busy, in the days that followed
you decided to paint portraits
of your flatmates.
I was flattered to be first.

Through my sitting you talked of Roddy,
took huge bites from oranges between strokes,
citrus juice staining your brushes and canvas,
and sat with your feet half buried by a mess of peel.

Now, when I slice into an orange,
I think of the picture, lost in some move or other,
and my face with the eyes you had given me,
the eyes of another man.

# Your Poem

*after Maurice Riordan's 'Frost'*

On the journey home I read your poem
and felt bad for not having read it before we met.
But of course it was too late to tell you
how much the poem meant to me
because I did not have your number.

The email that I'm sending this morning
about your poem will not quite convey
the feelings I had in the moment
that I read the poem, but perhaps
sometimes second is best;
and all we can hope for.

# Zones of Comfort

When we dared to go outdoors
we found a thousand leaves turned fish,
cast by the storm into puddles
the clay could not cope with.

Straining in the wind that lingered
these fish-leaves flip-flopped,
like the time the tank was broken;
on a soaking carpet life gasped away.

Then we saw the fence,
slapped down by the storm.
*Flat on the ground it's no use to anyone,*
said the man next door.
So we put the thing back up:
kept the man shut out,
kept ourselves shut in.

# The Mombasa Business

Hot belly of Mombasa;
business complete.
Stuck, hours waiting
for a ferry across
ferrous waters and home.

Or it feels like hours;
locked inside an ancient jeep.
Windows shut, tight.
Each twitch creating heat,
I fight to stay still.

A boy slams against the window.
I follow advice, avert my eyes.
Again. The slam against the glass.
Something forces me to look.
The boy's face tells us
this business is too big for us all.

# Surface Tension

Like emerging from anaesthetic
I watch in silence.
The screen shows mobile phones
passed around strangers
making comforting calls.
While below, casualties scroll
and fatalities grow.

In the room where I sit
my daughter blows a bubble;
it hovers above the set,
my eyes move to wonder
at the oil light lustre.

Caught between the air and gravity
this perfect globe collapses.
Tensions are too great,
a thousand specks of colour scatter.

She shrieks in delight,
wondering what happened.

# Staying the Night

A three legged bed,
copies of *The Times World Atlas* as props.
Windows that don't open, sealed by paint.
You say, *I hope there's no fire in the night.*
I'm thinking, *I hope the world can support us.*

## Arles, 1992

We slept until the sun snagged our eyes.
We poured our days away
in cheap wine beside the pool,
listening to Euro-pop radio
puzzled by voices too quick for us to follow.

The day we made it into town
you argued in the market place
with boys who whistled and made gestures.
You pulled me close
and I stoppered your anger with a kiss.

You always said that you'd go back.
The cartoon colours bring your vivid heat.
I put the postcard on the fridge
and wonder when those flowers turned to seed.

# After Sun

We pack our paperbacks away,
wet towels and costumes too.
The sky is now the colour
of the seals we watched
this morning in the bay.

The weather is broken:
jacketed we huddle,
rockpooled in silence,
rueing the change.

Dark coins pit the sand.
If we sit here long enough
we'll be washed away.
The gulls know what is coming
and fly inland.

# End of the Pier

Too scared to go on,
her stopping point was always
where the shingle became water,
while he strolled on—
out to the end of the pier.

Year on year she'd watch him recede,
passing the rides and amusement arcades,
his stooping gait, hands behind back—
until he was suspended at the furthest point.

And that is how it was.
He at one end
she at the other.

# Nostalgia Lesson

Like damp on the lungs
nostalgia gets into your heart.

You never learn your lesson,
cannot resist going back.

There you find feelings
and moments once had.

Half buried you pull them from silt;
their fossilised shapes are familiar

but such hard glassy surfaces
won't let you in.

# Tired of London

If we were new to loving
we'd find Parisian splendour all around.

We'd think this rain romantic
and wouldn't feel the lock iron cold.
Smoking outside between courses
would be charming and chic.

Montmartre and the Champs Elysees
are sepia to me.
London is grey, and we have loved too long.

# 3.7 cm (or 1.48 inches) Every Year

I learnt from the BBC
the moon is moving away from Earth
at a rate of 3.7 cm every year.

In Greenland coconuts will grow
while Vegas gambles six months under snow,
surfers will look to catch Saharan waves,
and only at high noon will bats return to caves.

There'll be no Hunter's, Harvest or half moon
but you may just sense things slide across the room.

This is what I learnt
just after you had rung.

Weightless,
spinning while you begin to fade.

# Testimony

A yellow sign
at the edge of the road
asks if anybody saw
a person falling from a car.

I don't know where to put
the memories of that night;
tracks scorched into my body,
in blood-black bruises
and bones that do not move.

How to explain
the storming that engulfed
us? I have no language
to express the way the eye
in which we lived
snapped shut.

Foot down, powering on,
you got away,
left me kerbside,
foetal, roadkill.

# I'm Not The Only One

In the post office I smell burning,
the kind you get when a pan boils dry.
I wonder if the lady behind the counter has noticed it,
but when I ask she just smiles and continues
leafing through papers.
Perhaps the Perspex screen between us
means she cannot smell the smell
that I think is getting stronger.
I imagine all the forms and banknotes, the stamps
and letters in the building going up
in flame, slowly spiralling into the sky
like sixty thousand bats anxious to escape
a dazzling sunrise in slow-motion.

I pop into the chemist,
where I still smell the burning.
The pharmacist gives me my prescription
and nods when I describe for him
what could happen to those seventy eight
tactile bottles of perfume, shaped with the curves
of a woman's body, if they meet with fire.

No one on the bus seems to notice
this burning smell either,
and I have in my head five images
of buses on fire that I have seen on television.

So when you get home and shriek
and say that my clothes are on fire,
I will be relieved to find someone
who smells burning too — otherwise
people might think that I am going mad.

# Earth Eater

My mud-scoffed mouth won't move,
so cram-full it is
with earth I've eaten.
I crumble my reaction
to all the kinds I've taken.

I enjoy the way,
like marbled steak that's turned,
blue-grey London clay
clags the palette and fugs my words.

I love loam; the way it slides
into the gut with fertile warmth
leaves me drunk.

I've been eating the land,
a pig, snaffling
until I've had my fill.

I lie back, sun-bake
or melt in rain
absorbed.

# Cow

How can I resist your pendulous hot heavy bags grown hard,
promise of so much goodness,
or your slow *look at me* sashay, your vibrating low,
the way you lie down to tell me the weather will break,
your boulder brown eyes, your slow rumination,
your tonnage of tongue
swept across that great big stupid dish face?
Beautiful cow, I can't resist
and there's no point even in pretending.

# Flatpack

My flatpack life has started to take shape,
though it looks nothing like the picture on the box.
The instructions are just diagrams
that make no sense, whichever way I hold the page.
Friends suggest I start again,
rubberneckers laugh.

But it functions, it stands up.
I don't care Tab B will not insert.
I've learnt the ways to improvise.

# Know Yourself

Calculate the square root of all moles.
Divide this number by the sum of skin tags found,
now multiply by the surface area of scar tissue.
Next, subtract the broken hearts, the kidney stones
and hernia to find the answer.
Think of a number and double it.

# Descaling

In beige afternoons, when I feel
fur growing around my strawberry heart,
I put a radio on to hear songs other people know.
I like travel news best—all those places
that can't be reached because of lorries broken down,
shed loads and over-running roadworks—
Snake Pass, Simister Island, Hog's Back.

Then I start descaling:
by the time I've rearranged the kitchen drawer,
taken leaking batteries from a torch,
thrown out the pile of unread daily papers,
my heart is no longer muzzled
and the roads have cleared.

# Horse Drawn

The sadness on the faces of the horses
that stand by the hedge separating
field from A-road, scurve my journey
and swarm in my sleep.

To stand all day and watch
is not enough;
such soul deep sorrow that
grows between folds of skin,
then spreads to take over the being,
can only hint at what is known.

In my rear view mirror
heads move, nostrils flare.
Some days I see myself
staring from amongst them.

# Not One Of Us

The moment that our bid became the winner
we christened her Loretta.
Two days later, she slid off the flatbed van
and came straight into our home.

She filled the hallway; huge hands, black fur
and such lovely life-like eyes.
Whenever we squeezed past to reach the door
we'd think of Attenborough and smile.

The children dressed Loretta
in hats and scarves, made blankets into a shirt.
I liked the way that she was always there
to meet me when I came in from work.

Then one day I opened the front door
to find ten billion tiny flies
had hatched from underneath Loretta's ear;
fur rippling and the air a shivering cloud of nightmare.

Fondness for Loretta vanished there and then—
we resented her betrayal
that led to pest control, new carpets
and phantom itching red of our own skins.

We decided on a bit of payback,
so that night Loretta burnt bright blue and chemical
when we struck a match and cursed
her back where she belonged.

# In Our Path

There wasn't anything more we could do—
the kitten noosed by orange wire lay dead
against the works where a team had fixed a leaking pipe.

Before we lay it beneath leaves
in a peaty shallow, you held the body
with the same care you had cradled Daniel
on that morning when everything changed.

# Glad Tidings

You are the maligned magnificent.
Iridescent. That green purple sheen
hinting at depths beneath
the black and white; your signature
so singular that only half a glance
tells me you are near.

Yours is lustrous beauty
reaching to the point
of those sleek tail feathers
that give such poise,
before you fan them open—
every card an ace.

But your appearance belies
the machine gun rattle exchange,
growing soundtrack to suburban life.
What is it that disturbs you?
What is it that you want?
Why have you come?

# Colouring Book

A blue dog beside a green cow,
the world my son creates is all his own.
To him the grass is red.

He bends the laws of nature
yet does his best to stay within
the confines of the printed shapes.

With rigid concentration
his tongue works upon his lower lip,
hands stiffened to ensure
the colours do not blur.

A beige dog beside a brown cow.
I stay within the lines,
my world obeys all natural laws.
To me the grass is always green.

# Garden Time

*A big stick is what you need.*
I remember saying that as he hacked about
the garden of our first home,
armed with just a pair of shears.

The house had stood so long deserted
it was hard to know just where to start;
inside or out, back or front?
Wherever we began, the work was hard and wearing.
Every evening we collapsed into each other's company,
and spoke of where the paths we made would lead.

Well, I had just remarked about the stick
when he then shouted *Snake!*
From under the compost heap it came,
two foot in length at least;
a green brown blur that slid beneath the shed.
*There's more life in this garden
than we had dreamt*, he said.
And so we left an area to grow wild
and shifted our attention to the rest.

# At Home

Warm and home,
just as it should be.
Sprawling upon the sofa
we are too tired to think
of anything beyond our door.

Content in our own company,
we welcome the fact
that this is where the past has put us.
Pushing tomorrow from our minds
we savour this moment like wine.

Sooner or later,
with my arm about your neck going numb,
we shift our positions
then settle once more
into our soft evening of love.

# I Never Noticed

Or like the time I was reading
in the bay window,
late one October afternoon;
you came in and said,
*How can you read in this?*

It was only then I saw
that gloom had settled in.
I tried to find my place
but all was blurred.

Somehow light had gone.
I hadn't slept or turned my back
but I didn't notice
our room becoming black.

# Butterfly Test

In bed we make a butterfly:
as if the sheet's been folded down the middle
we lie spine to spine, knees and elbows out at angles,
mirrored in the dark.

And before we sleep
you stare into our future while I stare into mine.
Or perhaps we make a Rorschach test—
tell me what you see.

# The Fish and the Jay

Kick out the clichés about birds;
flight, freedom, sky.
Forget any notion that they are
what we cannot be.
Focus instead upon
the dead jay I found in a pond.
Entangled with weed, and wire
mesh to keep the herons off,
it found itself surprised
by the weight of the water.
In terror it must have beaten its wings
against the strands that clung,
until the fight was gone
and only the slowness of time
and suffering mocked the bird to its end.

I dug a hole and with the shovel
lifted the dead thing dripping.
Stiffly it slid from the spade
into its peaty nest;
the blues and auburns were faded —
the way colours of the fish I kept
dulled when interest in them was gone;
I let the tank fur up;
through a green scum you had to peer,
to find the creatures
stiff upon their sides.

Your feet are bleeding from
pulling at the wire around them.
My head is bruised
and the glass won't break.

# Surfacing

I'm dredging for dreams;
swimming back along sleep's corridor
beneath a shower's hot membrane
searching for traces to guide me.

Concentration is everything—
day is pushing on the skin of dreams;
one false thought and in rushes
work, time, money.
A diver surfacing too fast
will be crushed.

In the shallows I snatch glimpses:
the car park swimming pool,
my father waiting. I might get back
as far as a face from school.

I take measurements
of flexing images,
bank them for analysis,

then push the button,
so they drain away,
as I catapult into the day.

# Being Dinner

Flat on the kitchen counter;
to your left, each night,
a figure in chef's whites sharpening a knife.
You suspected this ending.

You might be devoured whole—
tolerable given the circumstance.
Otherwise you may be sliced into strips
and fed to the dogs.

All you can hope for is speed.
You may be slow cooked for days
until the flesh falls away -
tender enough for babies to chew.

# Invisible

The thing that's grown inside me
cannot be explored by ultra-sound,
or removed by surgeon's knife.

I go to work as normal.
It exists inside my gut
and mind: controlling.

To leave the house in haste cannot be done.
First I feed the gnawing devil with ritual;
kettle, cooker, lights, taps,
switches, back-door. Kettle, cooker,
lights, taps, switches, back-door.

It wants more.
Plaster cracking is subsidence,
unknown emails contain viruses.
I cannot pay by phone
or order online just in case.

Awake at night to the electric thrum,
sweating to think of what comes next.
No scan can show this demon.
No lump can be removed.

# A letter to oneself

Dear              ,

We, the undersigned, are very sorry
to inform you that your behaviour last night
leaves us with no choice but to terminate
your involvement in family gatherings
and similar social events;
this includes weddings and funerals.

Our reasons for this decision are similar
to those we gave when all invitations
to work-dos were withdrawn.

We take no pleasure in issuing
this statement, but urinating into a sink
is not acceptable.

You should not expect behaviour that involves
aggression, talk of a sexual nature
or voluminous political cant
to be tolerated.

We wish you well with the future,
though we do advise you
to arrange for all socialising
to take place in isolation.

Yours sincerely,

# Reading in a church hall

When Lance read the word *fuck*
from the poem he had written,
Rebecca walked out.

It was not the word
she objected to,
but the fact that the workshop
was in a room at the church.

Lance hadn't meant to offend:
it was only his second meeting,
and he thought it was okay
to use *fuck* in a poem.

# Cley Hill

In tall grass crickets sound, and moths are starting to rise.
We watch them lift and land on honeysuckle or wild jasmine.
We need to remember this.

With the care a newborn child demands,
you cup a slip of yellowed paper into hollowed hands
and smuggle this gift into mine,
silently, like the kiss of secret love.

A flickering against my palms;
the moth is testing the limits of this new dark.
Downhill we go, towards cars
that have their lights on now;
my hands before me,
in supplication to this night.

# Sense of May

*In Memoriam F.M*

In May I found that link.
A night of firsts repeated,
as though discovering a truth
that told me all I thought was right.
Questions from before became clear,
and that moment of needle upon vinyl
was back again. Aching, quick
but careful, like a patient longing,
or driving home from hospital with your new born.

# Stargazing

We are walking a Norfolk beach
beneath the darkest-brightest sky I've ever seen.
He points to the Plough, the Milky Way,
the Dog Star and Orion.
*Follow my finger to the North Star.*
Together we trace our way
across the Universe;
joining the dots as we go.

# The Appointment

This is just a Tuesday morning in July,
the sixty minutes you pay and display
will pass at the same rate as every
hour you have ever spent.

Planes above are preparing to land
in the way they always do,
while magpies guarding their latest find
are subject only to the pulse
of circadian rhythms.

Your experience will not stop traffic,
you will not feature in the headlines
come six o'clock. The appointment
you are about to attend will turn
only your world upside down.
No animals will be harmed
and all identities will be protected.

## Your name

comes through dust
and air to reach my ear
then zips into my head,
splits itself in two—
message to brain,
charge to the heart.

I try it inside my mouth;
feel its weight, its shape,
the curve of vowel across a consonant.
Then push air through puckered lips
to make the sound of sea;
before a final syllable -
satisfied release,
all breath spent.

*(for U.E.)*

# The Gaps

*after Paul Farley*

Lying on my belly at the side of the pond in the park,
staring past my reflection looking
for newts to catch.

My brother face down
with those boys on his back, an unopened conker
                                        pressed into his skin.

Pulling a glove from the dog's mouth I get caught in its grip.
Blood pours but I don't let go.

Me and Paul Ray in the centre of a circle—
the others all chanting 'FIGHT, FIGHT, FIGHT,' Miss Harrison arrives,
*Yes, you'd better scram.* Paul Ray's left choking up blood.

We use bread and milk to feed hedgehogs,
then one morning we find one
drowned in a tub.
                    When did they stop coming?

I'm at my uncle's door, unable to go into his house. A Dalmatian named Chad.
He snarls and barks when I go near. I have to go home.

In the coal bunker it's musty and dark.
The spiders are huge but I like it (mind your head).

At playtime I pull the cap off the kid in the year below. Of course he has no hair
and I can't forgive the boy I was.

Aunty Ivy, Aunty Muriel, Aunty Peggy (and Uncle Burt) all live next door—
none are related to me. In pink, yellow and blue housecoats
I can hear them call over the fence.

Paul Ray again.
The tight squeeze of my mother's hand at the sound of the smash
as he falls through plate glass in his rush to open the door.

We are on quilts
  at the top of the stairs
    ready to slide to the floor.
Later I'm feint:  dislocated  thumb.

It's me falling from the loft, landing on my back;
a jaffa cake to put things right between my heavy breathing.

After a party I'm being sick, I spent all afternoon finishing drinks
people put down. My brother lies next to me.

In my sister's bedroom there are frogs jumping
from out of the bucket we've set on her bed.
     Each of us was born in this room.

The hamster gives birth—
eight blind babies.
We must not touch,
or else mummy will eat her young.
  I accepted that fact but as I got older it became more bizarre.

A hot day and mum tells us Elvis is dead. I think I know who he is.
In fact I have the wrong man.
Winter and the light is on. The man on the radio tells us
John Lennon's been shot. I know who he is.

Grandpa Elder's Sunday visit.  A Mars bar cut into quarters.
His missing finger—blown off in the war.
Dad's bristles on my face. Then I'm upside down—over the banister
held by the ankles.

*Parallel Lines* or *News of The World*?
*Parallel Lines*.

Supercalifragilisticexpialidocious.
Spell it.
Adam and Eve and Pinch Me went down to the river to bathe.

In the bath I learn that the red disc of a birthmark
on my right calf, was sellotaped by God.